Sarah Winnemucca
A Princess for the People

Sarah Winnemucca
A Princess for the People

John L. Smith

KEYSTONE
CANYON PRESS

For Amelia, my brave little flower

KEYSTONE
CANYON PRESS

Publisher Alrica Goldstein
Copyeditor Paul Szydelko
Cover Designer Alissa Gates Booth
Cartographer David Stroud
Picture Research Catherine Magee

Keystone Canyon Press
2341 Crestone Drive
Reno, NV 89523

www.keystonecanyon.com

The publisher would like to thank the Nevada Historical Society, the
Nevada State Museum, Nevada State Parks, University of Nevada
Archives, and the Library of Congress for their kind permission to take
and reproduce photographs.

A Cataloging-in-Publication record for this title is available from the
Library of Congress.

ISBN 978-1-953055-00-2
EPUB ISBN 978-1-953055-02-6

Manufactured in the United States of America

Table of Contents

Author's Note

Sarah Winnemucca's life remains as intriguing and controversial today as it was more than 150 years ago. She was celebrated and scorned by the press, politicians, and the public. Through the passage of time she has been depicted both as a brave and selfless leader of her people, and as one whose efforts were co-opted by the dominant white culture at times to the detriment of the tribe.

The pages that follow do not argue that controversy, but try to celebrate Winnemucca's undeniably courageous efforts to call out injustice and improve the lives of her people as best she could in rapidly changing times.

It's also important to note that the people known currently as the Northern Paiute did not call themselves by that name. They referred to themselves as "the people" and had their own language and long and rich spiritual and cultural traditions that were challenged and changed against their will.

Timeline

1844   Sarah Winnemucca is born near Humboldt River, precise date unknown.

1844   US Army Captain John C. Frémont travels through Northern Paiute country, eventually befriends Captain Truckee, Sarah's maternal grandfather.

1848   Gold is discovered in California at Sutter's Mill, attracting thousands of miners, speculators, and settlers from the East. They often traveled across Northern Paiute land.

1851   Genoa (first called Mormon Station) is founded. Considered Nevada's oldest town.

1851   Captain Truckee leads of group of Northern Paiute to see the white settlements in California. Sarah reluctantly goes along.

1859   Silver and gold is discovered near Virginia City.

1860   Pyramid Lake War. Pony Express mail services crosses Northern Paiute land.

1861   Civil War begins.

1864   Sarah speaks at Sutcliffe's Music Hall in Virginia City.

1864   On October 31, Nevada becomes a state.

1865   Mud Lake Massacre; Civil War ends.

1868   Sarah is hired as an interpreter at Fort McDermit.

1872   Paiute are relocated to Malheur, Oregon Reservation.

1878   Bannock War

Map of Northern Nevada/California

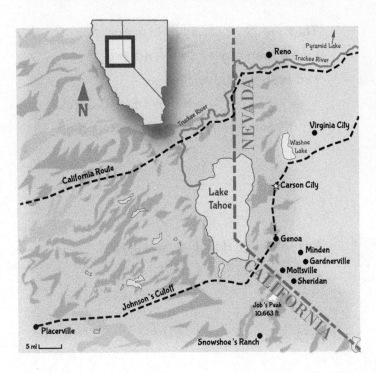

Thus we have clearly before us the white man's greed of land and the red man's lack of law.

> —Merrill Edwards Gates,
> US Board of Indian Commissioners 1885

Brave deeds don't always get rewarded in this world.

> —Sarah Winnemucca

Chapter One

A Girl Named Shell Flower

Before Nevada was a state, a girl was born into the Northern Paiute people who lived near the Humboldt River. Her proud parents named her Thocmetony ("Thoc-met-ony"), the Paiute word for the beautiful "Shell Flower" that signaled the promise of spring in the foothills of the Eastern Sierra Nevada mountain range.

They did not call themselves Paiute. They called themselves the Numa, which meant "the people." Outsiders called them Paiute (sometimes spelled Piute) to distinguish them from the Washo (also Washoe), Bannock, Shoshone (also Shoshoni), and other native people who lived in the region.

The Paiute had made their home in the long deserts, brush-covered foothills, and pinyon pine forests for many hundreds of years. When the summer sun beat hottest, the Numa moved up to the cool mountains. When the winter chill bit hardest, they followed the game down into the sunny valleys. They fished and hunted birds in Pyramid Lake and the

Humboldt River, harvested pine nuts in the mountains in late June, and hunted rabbit, deer, and pronghorn for meat to eat and dry as jerky, and for skins to make warm clothes for winter. They collected seeds and stored them to prepare for the coldest months. They even made tea out of pine nuts and used small stones taken from campfires to heat their water.

The Numa left nothing to waste. From the grasses near the lake they wove their sandals. They wove tule reeds into skirts and pine needles into baskets. They used the sticky sap from the pines for glue. They used stones to grind seeds and nuts into meal.

From the willow branches they made snares and traps for small animals and birds. They used the meat

While the Washoe people had a different culture and language, they used the same grasses and beeds to make jewelry and baskets that could be traded.

2

for food and the fur for blankets. From the bones of the birds they made flutes and smoking pipes. They used the feathers for their arrows and as decorations.

They knew different rocks served different purposes. Smooth, round grinding stones, called "manos," were found in riverbeds. The grinding bowl, called a "metate," was made of volcanic rock. Super-sharp spear points and arrowheads were chipped from glass-like jasper and obsidian.

The seasons were sometimes very hard, but there was enough food for the spiritual and peaceful Numa.

Their life began to change forever with the appearance of the first explorers and settlers. The explorers often traveled alone or in small groups in the mid-1820s. The settlers followed the explorers and arrived in small numbers on foot and horseback from the West and in large groups from the East in wagons pulled by oxen in the late-1840s. Some of the strangers had come seeking silver and gold.

Although the strangers had come from many places, they became known by their pale skin. The men's round, owlish faces were sometimes covered with hair, and they spoke a strange language.

Little Thocmetony was afraid. She had heard the Paiute story of "Cannibal Owl," who swooped down to snatch up and eat children who did not mind their parents.

Were these the Cannibal Owls? Would she be eaten, too? The thought frightened her. So did the never-ending numbers of strangers.

"I was a very small child when the first white people came into our country," she would remember many years later. "They came like a lion, yes, like a roaring lion, and have continued so ever since, and I have never forgotten their first coming."

She was told by her mother, Tuboitony (Tub-wa-tony), to hide from the white people, who did not understand and respect Paiute ways and were sometimes violent. One time, Tuboitony and her husband, Winnemucca, dug shallow holes and buried Sarah and her sister so that only their heads were exposed. They placed bushes around their heads to protect them from the sun and to add a final touch to their hiding place. The girls waited quietly for hours, holding back sobs, always in fear that strangers would come and harm them.

Thocmetony said, "Oh, father, have you forgotten me? Are you never coming for me?"

She cried so much she thought her heart would break.

When the danger passed, the children were very relieved. Finally, her mother and father returned and uncovered the girls.

"Oh, can anyone in this world ever imagine what were my feelings when I was dug up by my poor mother and father?" she wondered many years after that day.

Chapter Two

Hard Lessons and a New Language

Many Paiute were suspicious and afraid of the whites. But the little girl's maternal grandfather, Captain Truckee, who was the leader of the Northern Paiute people, embraced the newcomers as his long lost brothers. He believed that the whites and the Paiute could live together peacefully. Because he was a chief of the Numa, his views were widely respected.

Captain Truckee guided whites many times through the mountains into California, where he saw towns and cities filled with hundreds and thousands of the newcomers. His people helped feed desperate whites in winter. He even helped guide explorer US Army Captain John C. Frémont in a war against Mexico.

Captain Truckee returned to his tribe convinced that the Paiute needed to learn the ways of the white people, and so in 1851 he traveled to California with a group that included young Thocmetony. On the way, Thocmetony hid in fear whenever she saw the strangers.

US Army Captain John C. Frémont led expeditions into the American West.

In California, the little girl saw sights that included brick houses three-stories high and steamboats that billowed smoke and noisily moved up and down the San Joaquin River. She was amazed.

While in California, the six-year-old Thocmetony grew sick and covered with a rash from poison oak. A kind white woman helped her recover, and she began to realize that not all of the strangers were untrustworthy.

When the family returned to its home, Thocmetony and her younger sister were sent to Genoa to live with the family of Major William Ormsby. It was there that Thocmetony learned her first words of English. She took the name Sarah Winnemucca, and she made her first white friend, the Ormsbys' daughter, Lizzie Jane.

Sarah helped with household chores and served food to travelers to Genoa. In their spare time, Sarah and Lizzie went to square dances. By this time, young Sarah had long black hair and flashing dark eyes.

Sarah was learning to trust her new white friends, but she soon discovered that not all the newcomers were worthy of that trust. It was a lesson that would repeat itself throughout her life.

Pyramid Lake in Nevada is a remnant of ancient Lake Lahontan from the Pleistocene Epoch about two million years ago and home to many Northern Paiute even today.

Sarah and her younger sister, Elma, knew they were different. That much was obvious from the color of their skin and the style of their dress. But they were learning the new ways and, with help from the Ormsby family, learned to speak English.

Meanwhile, the violence between the settlers and the Paiute was growing. Captain Truckee knew the Paiute's future depended on their ability to live peacefully near the whites, but he needed to make his brothers understand Paiute ways.

Captain Truckee sent Sarah and Elma to the Sisters' School in San Jose, California, to learn to read and write. The girls were nervous, but they obeyed their wise grandfather. He understood that education was the most powerful tool to help the Numa.

It's been recorded that they were admitted into the school, but soon the other children's parents complained. The parents didn't want their children to associate with the brown-skinned girls.

Sarah and Elma were told they would have to leave. Indians were considered to be less than whites. The two girls returned to the land of the Paiute by stagecoach.

Sarah learned a hard lesson, but she didn't let the experience harden her heart.

Her brave heart and knowledge of English would soon be needed at home.

Chapter Three

The Pyramid Lake War

Sarah would recall how two miners named McMullen and MacWilliams were murdered in the mountains. Although the men had been shot and only their money was missing, Washoe arrows were placed by their bodies. Indians were suspected despite the fact the miners' food and belongings—items in short supply for the hungry people—were still in their camp.

When Major Ormsby arrived to investigate, Sarah's brother Natches attempted to reason with him. But Ormsby was convinced of the Washoe's guilt. After a meeting with the chief of the tribe, the Washoe were ordered to produce three men to stand for punishment. The men were innocent of the crimes, but to avoid greater bloodshed three Washoe men were made prisoners and handed over to the soldiers. Two were killed to pay a debt they did not owe.

Sarah railed at the injustice.

"This was the first trouble the poor Washoes had with white people, and the only one they ever did have with them," she recalled many years later. "So the day passed away, and the two dead Washoes were taken away, and their bodies were burned. That is their custom . . . My little sister made herself sick she cried so much that day."

Sarah's cousin Numaga was a tall man for his time. Standing six feet tall, with piercing eyes and a fluency in English, he was the Northern Paiute's war chief. Sarah's brother Natches was the tribe's peace chief. Both had challenging roles to play in the difficult months of 1859 when the Numa suffered greatly from a lack of food.

The Paiute, Bannock, and Shoshone felt the world they had known shrink with every settler, miner, and rancher who moved into the region. Their hunting and gathering grounds were depleted and they faced starvation in the harsh winter. Although some whites and army soldiers showed them empathy and shared food, others turned away.

Throughout the region there were incidents of violence. While Indians were sometimes guilty of violence, and of stealing cattle for food, they were also easy to blame for crimes they did not commit. And most whites made no distinction between Paiute clans, even those who were not friendly with each other. To the newcomers, one Indian was just like another—and all were to be feared. As chief, Winnemucca found himself blamed by the whites.

NA-MA'-GA, OR YOUNG WINNEMUCCA.

Numaga was the Northern Paiute's war chief during the starving year of 1859.

11

But the whites were also guilty of crimes. When two Paiute girls disappeared and tracks led to Williams Station on the Carson River, the two brothers who ran the trading post were suspected of kidnapping. But the girls could not be found.

As hostilities increased, the tribes in the area began to talk of war. Only Numaga stood against a fight that could not be won.

He tried to reason with the others, reminding them that "the white men are like the stars over your head" in their number. "You have wrongs, great wrongs, that rise up like those mountains before you; but can you, from the mountaintops, reach and blot out those stars. Your enemies are like the sands in the bed of your rivers; when taken away they only give place for more to come and settle there."

His powers of reason were strong, Sarah would later recall, but before he could resolve the call for war the council received word that the girls had been found at Williams Station. They had been physically abused. In retaliation, the Paiute killed the Williams brothers and three other men who had the misfortune of being at the trading post.

The chance for peace was lost.

In retaliation for the killing at Williams Station, Major Ormsby led a group of more than 100 poorly trained volunteer soldiers in an attempt to capture the Paiute. On May 12, 1860, near the Truckee River, the shabby soldiers followed a small group of Paiute into a trap. Dozens of volunteers were killed. Ormsby, whose friendly relationship with Winnemucca had enabled Sarah to receive an education, was also killed.

Major William Ormsby took Sarah into his family as a young girl.

The Paiute had won a battle Numaga had wanted to avoid because he knew the tribe and all its allies could not win the war. Within days more soldiers poured into the area, constructing Fort Churchill and showing a much greater presence. Numaga agreed to calm the hostilities, but only after the Numa's grievance was heard. The people were starving and desperate.

As the violence subsided, the Paiute lost its patriarch when Captain Truckee died after a long illness. He had been the one who welcomed the whites as brothers when he guided John C. Frémont as an explorer and in battle. He had been a great influence in Sarah's young life, and she mourned his death. His influence had led to Sarah seeking an education and learning English. She would eventually also learn Spanish and three Native American dialects, all by age fourteen. But at that moment, they spoke the universal language of grief.

"Everyone threw themselves upon his body, and their cries could be heard for many a mile," she recalled years later. "I could hardly believe he would never speak to me again. I knelt beside him and took his dear old face in my hands, and looked at him quite a while. I could not speak. I felt the world growing cold; everything seemed dark. The great light had gone out. . . . I was only a simple child, yet I knew what a great man he was. I mean great in principle. I knew how necessary it was for our good that he should live. I think if he had put out his hands and asked me to go with him, I would gladly have folded myself in his arms."

The Pyramid Lake War did not last long, but it had taken a toll on both sides. It also led Sarah to later exclaim that white charity was fleeting and rarely given without wanting something in return.

"During the winter my people helped them," she would write. "They gave them such as they had to eat. They did not hold out their hands and say: 'You can't have anything to eat unless you pay me.' No, no such word was used by us savages at that time."

She seemed to ask, "Just who were the real savages?"

Chapter Four

Sarah Takes the Stage

Not long after the end of the Pyramid Lake War, a far greater conflict broke out in the United States. The Civil War would last four years and cost an estimated 750,000 lives. While Abraham Lincoln was president, Nevada gained its statehood and became the thirty-sixth state on October 31, 1864.

As Nevada made the transition from territory to state, life for the Paiute changed little. Although they had lived in the area for centuries, they were not citizens of the state. They could not vote. And they increasingly found themselves competing for food and land that had access to water.

Nevada's population grew rapidly in the 1860s, from 6,857 at the start of the decade to 42,941 in 1870. That growth overwhelmed the native population and continued to lead to trouble. In the beginning the Paiute were willing to share their land and the animals that roamed on it with the whites, but by the time of statehood, deer and antelope were harder to find, and

Pronghorn were an important source of meat for the early inhabitants of the area.

even the rabbits were less plentiful.

As more whites arrived, they claimed more land and pushed the Paiute into smaller and smaller areas. In return for being able to stay in an area, known as a reservation, the Paiute were promised food, clothing, and tools for farming. Every promise by the US government was broken, and as the seasons passed the Paiute became hungrier and more desperate.

After Captain Truckee died, his son-in-law, Winnemucca, became chief. In 1864, Chief Winnemucca took his family to Virginia City to tell of the Paiute's hardship. By then, Virginia City had become Nevada's greatest boomtown with more than

Sarah's father, Chief Winnemucca, took his family
to Virginia City, Nevada, to tell of the Paiute's
hardship wearing a headress made of feathers.

15,000 people following the nearby discovery of silver
and gold in the Comstock Lode in 1859.

Her tribe's desperate circumstances and her ability
to speak English pushed Sarah into the spotlight.
Chief Winnemucca chose her to tell the Paiute's story

to the whites. The audiences were very impressed with Sarah's communication skills. While Chief Winnemucca wore a headdress made of feathers, Sarah interpreted his words to the whites. She spoke clearly, and the audiences at Sutcliff's Music Hall were impressed and entertained.

Although the Paiute dressed simply as a general rule, Sarah began wearing pretty beaded clothing to reflect what the white audiences imagined an Indian princess looked like. Sarah found that many people appreciated her way of speaking, her sincerity, and appearance. She would make more than 400 speeches in her lifetime. For many settlers, Sarah was the first Native person that they had seen in person.

She used the curiosity of the newspaper reporters to describe the plight of her people to thousands of readers. She gave many interviews and was considered not only a representative of her people, but a celebrity as well.

From Virginia City, Sarah and her family traveled to San Francisco and performed at the Metropolitan Theater. Sarah was very nervous. She became so flustered by the crowd that she sat down on the stage and exclaimed that she could not understand Chief Winnemucca's words. Charmed by her candor, the audience applauded wildly. But people were more entertained than educated about the plight of the troubled Paiute. The performances didn't help feed her people, but they gave Sarah the experience she would need to address more important audiences in the future.

Sarah only wore costumes like this
when presenting to white audiences.

Meanwhile, relations between the Paiute and the
white settlers were getting worse. The Paiute were
hungry. To feed the tribe, Paiute sometimes killed
animals that belonged to the settlers and ranchers.

Sarah suffered a great personal loss in March
1865 when soldiers from Camp McDermit led by an
inexperienced captain mistook a Paiute fishing and
gathering party camped at Mud Lake for cattle rustlers

and attacked them, killing twenty-nine men, women, and children. The ambush was cheered by white settlers in the area. Sarah's mother, Tuboitony, and one of her baby brothers were killed in the attack. Sarah's sister, Elma, barely escaped on horseback and was considered the only survivor of the slaughter.

"Oh, it is a fearful thing to tell, but it must be told," she would write years later. "Yes, it must be told by me. It was all old men, women, and children that were killed. After the soldiers had killed all but some children and babies still tied up in their baskets, the soldiers took them also, and threw them into the flames to see them burned alive."

The memory of the Mud Lake Massacre would never leave her heart as she continued to improve the lives of her people.

Chapter Five

A Letter from Sarah

Sarah knew from experience that her people could not defeat the whites in war. For the Paiute to survive, the two different cultures must manage to coexist. But how?

She tried to speak truth to the white world about the condition of her people at a time many believed that Indians were uncivilized savages who were dangerous, lazy, dirty, ignorant, and unteachable. White settlers and cattle ranchers commonly pushed out the Numa with their expanding towns and grazing herds. The fact that the Paiute had their own language, culture, religion, and a storytelling tradition that reached back centuries was rarely considered when settlers looked at their humble ways.

She decided to use her ability to speak and write in English, a rare skill among her people at that time, to challenge the government's Indian agents and point out their deception and corruption. In April 1870, she wrote a letter to US Army Major Henry Douglas, the superintendent of Indian Affairs for Nevada, explaining the plight of the Paiute. At the time, Douglas was considering sending the Paiute to the Truckee River Reservation, which was bitterly cold in winter.

She explained that she was the daughter of the elderly Paiute Chief Winnemucca. She then criticized the living conditions at the Truckee reservation and wrote that life was made worse because the government agents in charge of the reservation refused to provide the tribe with blankets and enough food. She wanted Douglas to know her people preferred to remain at Camp McDermit, where they received food and clothing, than to be forced onto a reservation where, "if we had stayed there, it would be only to starve." Her criticism was considered very bold.

"I think that if they had received what they were entitled to from the agents, they would never have left them," Sarah wrote.

She also questioned the government's decision to issue the Paiute seed without explaining basic agriculture. Farming on a larger scale was new to them. Sarah raised a subject that, in its way, exposed the ignorance of both sides. The Paiute had, she wrote, "never had the opportunity of learning; but I think, if proper pains were taken, that they would be willing to make the effort to maintain themselves by their own labor, providing they could be made to believe that the products were their own, for their own use and comfort."

She then moved on to the challenges of surviving while being restricted to a reservation.

"It is needless for me to enter into details as to how we were treated on the reservation while there," she wrote. "It is enough to say that we were confined to the reserve, and had to live on what fish we might be able to catch in the river. If this is the kind of civilization awaiting us on the reserves, God grant that we may never be compelled to go on one, as it is much preferable to live in the mountains and drag out an existence in our native manner. So far as living is concerned, the Indians at all military posts get enough to eat and considerable cast-off clothing."

Then she did something unheard of from an Indian—much less an Indian woman. She challenged the major to do something about it.

"But how long is this to continue?" she wrote. "What is the object of the Government in regard to Indians? Is it enough that we are at peace? Remove all the Indians from the military posts and place them on reservations such as the Truckee and Walter River Reservations . . . and it will require a greater military force stationed round to keep them within the limits than it now does to keep them in subjection."

Making her argument stronger, Sarah didn't just complain of the poor conditions. She offered a possible long-term solution, one she would promote the rest of her life: workable land set aside for the Paiute to create their own homes.

"On the other hand," she wrote, "if the Indians have any guarantee that they can secure a permanent home on their own native soil, and that our white neighbors can be kept from encroaching on our rights, after having a reasonable share allotted to us as our own, I warrant that the savage (as he is called today) will be a thrifty and law-biding member of the community fifteen or twenty years hence."

She also offered to work with the major and share her knowledge of the Paiute so that he could better understand them.

When Major Douglas read Sarah's words, they moved him to share the letter with others. A copy of the letter was published in one local newspaper, then others in the area. Before long, a San Francisco newspaper republished the letter from the literate young Paiute woman who spoke out so clearly and critically about the treatment they were receiving by their white brothers.

In time, the letter made its way to New York and the offices of the respected and widely read *Harper's* magazine, which first began publishing in 1850 and is still in print today.

Sarah's letter to Major Douglas is among the earliest publication of writing by an Indian woman. Its message echoed far beyond her humble home at Fort McDermit. In time, Sarah's name and the plight of the Paiute would be known throughout the United States.

Chapter Six

The Malheur Dream

As American settlers continued to populate the West, and the cattle and sheep ranching grew to an enormous scale, clashes between the whites and the Indians increased and became a greater concern to federal officials in Washington, DC. In an attempt to end the violence and make more room for the newcomers, in 1872 President Ulysses S. Grant ordered the creation of the vast Malheur Reservation for use as a homeland to "all the roving and straggling bands (of Indians) in Eastern and Southeastern Oregon, which can be induced to settle there." To the Paiute, who suffered from a lack of food, the 1.7-million-acre reservation seemed like a dream-come-true.

While Sarah was already well known as the Paiute Princess who spoke English and made numerous public appearances in Sacramento and San Francisco, her heart remained with her people. Sarah was suspicious of the Malheur Reservation and preferred the known world of Fort McDermit. But in time the numbers of

Paiute, Bannock, Shoshone, and other tribes grew in the new country. The Northern Paiute living at what was once called Camp McDermit and other military installations were slow to accept the change. Sarah, her brother Natches and her aging father, Winnemucca, moved to Fort Harney near Malheur in 1875. Game was abundant, and the plants and seeds the Paiute ate in their diets were plentiful. And there was something else that must have made the place seem like a dream come true: a reservation agent who showed genuine concern about the Numa. His name was Samuel Parrish.

Parrish, she believed, was a good man who endeavored to understand the ways and needs of the Indians. The Indians respected him, but many settlers who sought land in the reservation scorned him.

When Sarah arrived at Fort Harney, she was asked to act as an interpreter and at first was distrustful. But after meeting Parrish, she came away impressed. He not only was willing to teach the Paiute new farming skills, but he promised to buy what they grew at a fair price. She would later recall Parrish telling a group of tribal leaders, "I will try and do my duty, and teach you all how to work, so you can do for yourselves by and by."

And he kept his promise.

"So my people went with a good heart, both old men and young women and children," Sarah recalled. "We were happy as could be."

Parrish taught the Indians how to bring water to their fields by building dams and irrigation ditches. He taught them how to build strong fences to keep animals from ruining the crop. He not only gave them the skills to succeed, but the incentive to go with it: what they grew was theirs to sell or keep. They worked hard, brought water to 120 acres, and their fields flourished.

Next came the construction of a schoolhouse, where Parrish's sister-in-law Annie would teach the Paiute children with help from Sarah's ability to translate. More progress was made. It seemed another dream, the education of the next generation of Paiute, was being realized.

Sarah settled in as a teacher's assistant, acting as an interpreter for the children and Annie. The children responded to the teaching strategy. "They learn very fast, and were glad to come to school," she observed. "I cannot tell or express how happy we were!" They were productive days for Sarah and the Numa.

But as before, settlers and ranchers continued to encroach on the new reservation. They made claims on the land and accused Parrish of siding with the Paiute. With the help of Parrish and US Army Major John Green, the Indians won a brief victory.

It did not last.

Despite a letter sent on Parrish's behalf from the Paiutes, along with the support of Major Green and his commanding general, O. O. Howard, public opinion was turning against the Indians again. As newcomers took land that the Paiute had known as their home for generations, the Paiute sometimes responded with violence. News of Indian battles with settlers and the army echoed throughout the West. The ranchers seeking to expand their range onto the Malheur Reservation used their political allies in Washington and eventually succeeded in removing Parrish from his position. That left the Paiute vulnerable.

William V. Rinehart, who had a terrible temper and made his disgust for the Indians well known, replaced the kind and fair Parrish. Rinehart especially hated Sarah's father, Winnemucca, who was sometimes called "Bad Face." He cancelled previous agreements that enabled the Indians to profit from their labor, instead promising to pay them a meager dollar a day for their labor, and then cheated them out of that. The Indians protested, but the dark-hearted Rinehart told them that if they didn't like the new rules they could leave.

Sarah saw the changes taking place and took her complaints about Rinehart public. In private, leaders of the different bands of Indians living at Malheur Reservation met to discuss what to do next. They were growing more desperate by the day. Rinehart punished them by shorting their rations of food. Agents at other reservations in the region did the same.

It became clear to them that Rinehart was trying to drive them away so that the ranchers and settlers could make use of the reservation land. Sarah took the tribes' complaints against Rinehart to Camp Harney and Major Green, who had helped them previously.

Chapter Seven

The Bannock War

By the spring of 1878 the Paiute were starving and
had grown weary of the agents stealing the wages
they had earned and the food and materials they had
been promised. Talk of war grew among the Bannock
and some Paiute, but Winnemucca risked his own life
to counsel against it. He warned that they were far
outnumbered. To show the difference he scooped two
piles of sand, one large and one small, next to each
other. Pointing to the small pile, he said, "This Indian.
No use to fight." The army was too great, he reminded
those who wanted war, and the Indians were too
few. But he was losing the battle of words. And then
Winnemucca lost his freedom when the Bannocks took
him and his band of braves prisoner.

Hired by the army at Fort McDermit to locate the
Bannock war party, Sarah and a few scouts rode hard
on horseback north fifty miles or more a day. Sarah
was an excellent rider, and she pressed on despite
the danger, reaching the edge of the war camp and

learning of her people's capture. With help from her brother Lee, she devised a plan to sneak into the Bannock camp, a place where she would surely be killed if her identity were discovered.

"I must save my father and his people if I lose my life in trying to do it, and my father's too," she told her brother. "That is all right. I have come for you all. Now let us go."

Climbing through the high rocks by night, she looked into a valley where an estimated 500 warriors camped— and where Winnemucca and some of his family were held captive. While the Bannocks ate their evening meal, she sneaked into her father's lodge. Sarah told them of the approaching danger and the need to escape. A plan was devised. The Paiute women would slip away while supposedly out gathering wood, the children with them.

Once they left camp after dark, Sarah would remember in her autobiography, they climbed through the night despite their fatigue. "It was like a dream," she wrote. " . . . I almost fell down at every step, my father dragging me along."

When they reached their horses, they rode many miles with the murderous Bannock on their trail. They rested only briefly, slept little and ate and drank less. They were exhausted when they returned to the soldiers after only three days. They had ridden more than 200 miles in that short time.

She would later remember with pride, "I went for the government when the officers could not get an Indian or a white man to go for love or money. I, only an Indian

Horses were brought to the North American continent by the Spanish in the early 1500s. By the mid-1800s, more than two million ran wild and now over half of the wild horses left live in Nevada.

woman, went and saved my father and his people."

Once she reported to General Howard, she was hired as a guide and interpreter. It was not easy for her to work for the army in a war against the Indians, even those who sought to harm her family. She understood their anger, and she had known their hunger.

For the next few weeks in the summer of 1878, Sarah assisted General Howard in the campaign against the Bannocks and some Paiutes. The Indians were no match for the army, although there was terrible violence and much bloodshed on both sides. After two months in battle, Sarah said goodbye to the general. While her services were no longer needed, he would remember her and praise her service for the rest of his life.

But there was more work to do. To the north, in Oregon, an Umatilla tribe war party had captured Paiute women and children. Sarah immediately joined in the plan to rescue them. They succeeded not in secret, but after brother Natches embarrassed and shamed them in public. The women and children were released. With them the Paiute returned to Fort McDermit to remain under the army's protection until they were again ordered to move despite the cold season.

The Bannock War was brief, but it scattered the Paiute. More than 500 Indians were taken prisoner and herded north to the Washington Territory and Yakama Reservation. To the army officers, Sarah was an irreplaceable hero. To those Indians who had fought in the Bannock War, she was an unforgivable enemy. Hundreds of captured warriors were imprisoned at Yakama Reservation more than 500 miles across a landscape growing colder by the day. The Paiute had no permanent home and were being pushed from Fort McDermit back north to Malheur Reservation and Fort Harney, where the callous Rinehart was in charge. Once at the Yakama Reservation, they were treated poorly and struggled to survive. It was a terrible time for the Paiute. Had it really been only two years since those good days under the friendship of Samuel Parrish?

Throughout it all, she remained an invaluable resource to her people and to the military.

At Vancouver Barracks in the Washington Territory (it was not yet a state,) Sarah worked as an

32

THE WESTERN UNION TELEGRAPH COMPANY.

The rules of this Company require that all messages received for transmission, shall be written on the message blanks of the Company, under and subject to the conditions printed thereon, which conditions have been agreed to by the sender of the following message.

WILLIAM ORTON, Pres't, | NEW YORK.
A. R. BREWER, Sec'y,

Dated *Portland, April 19* 187*8*

Received at _____ 2P.

To *Commanding Officer*
Fort Vancouver.

*Issue such clothing as
may be necessary to make
the Prisoners of war cleanly
and respectable —
Any essential purchase
for the women prisoners will
be approved.*
(Sig) Rec'd apl 19/78

*Howard
Com'g*

31 Pd
= S. Co3. =

In places like Vancouver Barracks in 1878, the fastest communications
were sent over telegraph wires and handwritten on pages like the one above.

interpreter and teacher. "In this capacity, she always
gave abundant satisfaction to all who were interested in
Indian children," General Howard recalled.

US Army Lieutenant Colonel Edwin Mason, who served under Howard, was even more lavish in his praise, recounting how Sarah served a "valuable service" as a scout and interpreter. "After the capture of the 'hostiles' she devoted herself to the interests of her people . . . going with them from Fort Harney, Oregon, to the Yakama Reservation, then to Washington City, ever intent on trying to accomplish something for their good. I have known Sarah Winnemucca a number of years and have never known her to do or say a thing that was not perfectly upright and womanly. She is honest, true, faithful, and worthy of respect and the esteem of all good people. I earnestly recommend her to the kindly regard of all who wish well to her race."

In 1879, the dream of a common homeland for the Paiute and other tribes in the region ended. Rinehart, who had displayed such contempt for Sarah and her people, was successful in discontinuing Malheur Reservation.

In its way, it was one of the war's greatest casualties.

Sarah's heart ached for her people, but what could she do to help them?

She could only speak her truth using the language and writing she had learned. And so she did. Sarah again took their case to white society and made a plea for justice for the Numa. In November 1879, she traveled with Natches and other relatives to San Francisco to speak to audiences about the Bannock War and the condition of the Paiute. The audiences cheered her impassioned speeches.

Chapter Eight

Promises Made, Promises Broken, and a Petition to Congress

The Paiute were scattered widely after the Bannock War. Some were held in Washington at Yakama Reservation and Fort Vancouver, others remained in Nevada at Fort McDermit. While many would have liked to return to Malheur Reservation, few were willing to go anywhere near a place where the cruel agent Rinehart was in charge.

Sarah spoke out often in her attempt to gain support for the Paiute's plight and reunite the tribe. She knew the final decision would have to come from the authorities in Washington, DC. And so in the late fall of 1879 she implored General Howard to write a letter of recommendation to the Indian Commissioner's Office in the nation's capital on her behalf. The general was grateful to Sarah for her courageous efforts during the Bannock War and respected the devotion she had for improving the lives of her people. He knew the Paiute were a peaceful people buffeted by hunger and great change most could not comprehend. On November 7, he wrote not one letter, but two on Sarah's behalf.

The first note endorsed her character and efforts during the war to ease in her safe passage to the East. It read in part, "I have promised to put in writing some opinion as to your capabilities, and it gives me great pleasure to state that during the Bannock campaign of 1878, and also later, you have displayed an unusual intelligence and fearlessness, and loyalty to the whites in your capacities of scout, interpreter, and influential member of the Paiute tribe of Indians. Probably very few people will ever know how much credit is due you for a successful ending of the war in the surrender of the hostile members of your tribe."

On another sheet of paper he wrote to General E. Whittlesey of the Board of Indian Commissioners: "Please do what you can to assist Sarah Winnemucca to have a fair interview . . . should her people send her to Washington. She was of the greatest assistance to us in the campaign of 1878, and has since been working hard for her people. They are on the Yakama Reservation partly—partly on the Warm Springs Reservation, and the remainder in Nevada, near Fort McDermit."

It was a very promising start.

She traveled back to Washington with a small group to plead for relief for the Numa. Hope rode with her. A meeting with Secretary of the Interior Carl Schurz held promise. Appointed by President Rutherford B. Hayes, Schurz was in charge of all federal lands in the West and was known as a reformer of the government's hostile treatment of Native Americans. Like so many politicians before and since, he was known for saying one thing and doing another.

For the meeting with Schurz, Natches spoke up in their native language with Sarah translating. After acknowledging the power of the "Great Father," Natches said, "There is nothing you can't do if you wish to; and, therefore, we one and all, pray you give us back what is of no value to you or your people. Oh, good father, it is not your gold, nor your silver, horses, cattle, lands, mountains we ask for. We beg of you to give us back our people, who are dying off like so many cattle, or beasts, at the Yakama Reservation."

When Natches and Sarah were finished, Schurz must have been impressed by their passion for their fellow Paiute. Sarah certainly was a well-spoken and confident woman unafraid to challenge one of the most powerful men in America. After the meeting, Schurz gave his word and a letter that the Paiute could return to the Malheur Reservation. The secretary would make sure each family received tents in which to live, and Sarah would receive a good job as an interpreter at the reservation.

It seemed like a great breakthrough. Sarah was heartened. She couldn't wait to get back to the West and tell the people of the good news. She made public appearances in Washington, and two days after speaking with Schurz she was given a meeting with President Hayes. It was considered a great honor for anyone to receive such a meeting, and Sarah had high expectations of being in the presence of the great man.

The meeting was brief, she later recalled in her autobiography, and the president asked her if she had received "all you want for your people." She thought a moment and replied, "Yes, sir, as far as I know."

She believed she had gone as far as she could go to impress upon the highest authority under heaven of the need for her people to be reunited in a place they could call their own. She rushed to return and tell the Paiute the good news.

Winnemucca, Natches, and Sarah spread out to explain what they had been told by Schurz and the president himself.

"Just think how happy I was to go for my poor, sick-hearted people. Yes, armed with a paper signed by Secretary Schurz. I thought I would not have anything to do but go there and get them."

But she was mistaken.

The people were elated at first to hear the good news. But as the weeks passed and the promised official word from Washington did not come, they began to grow suspicious. Not only of the president, but of Sarah herself.

She grew angry and in future public appearances that voice of protest became louder. In Boston, she attracted the attention of the writer, publisher and social reformer Elizabeth Peabody and her sister, the editor Mary Peabody Mann. They would become important influences in Sarah's life.

Sarah kept on fighting for her people. In 1883, she circulated a petition to Congress calling for the return of her people to the Malheur reservation. She included

PETITION

To the Honorable Congress of the United States.

Whereas, the tribe of Piute Indians that formerly occupied the greater part of Nevada and now diminished by its sufferings and wrongs to one-third of its original number, has always kept its promise of peace and friendliness to the whites since they first entered their country, and has of late been deprived of the Malheur Reservation decreed to them by President Grant:

I, Sarah Winnemucca Hopkins, granddaughter of Captain Truckee, who promised friendship for his tribe to General Fremont, whom he guided into California and served through the Mexican war — together with the undersigned friends who sympathize in the cause of my people — do petition the Honorable Congress of the United States to restore to them said Malheur Reservation, which is well watered and timbered, and large enough to afford homes and support for them all, where they can enjoy lands in severalty without loosing their tribal relations, so essential to their happiness and good character, and where their citizenship, implied in this distribution of land, will defend them from the encroachments of the white settlers, so detrimental to their interest and their virtues. And especially do we petition for the return of that portion of the tribe arbitrarily removed from the Malheur Reservation, after the Bannock war, to the Yakima Reservation, on Columbia River in which removal families were ruthlessly separated, and have never ceased to pine for husbands, wives, and children, which restoration was pledged to them by the Secretary of the Interior in 1880, but has not been fulfilled.

Original documents like this petition are important research tools. In this one, Sarah asks that her people be returned to the Malheur Reservation.

letters from Elizabeth Peabody and some of the army officers she had served.

In her letter, Peabody urged the committee to give the land at Fort McDermit to the Paiute in the name of self-sufficiency and human decency. "If done at once," she wrote, "it will be cheaper for the government and save the tribe from quite perishing. Without a home, & with no conditions of self-support, they appeal to the heart of the humane irresistibly."

On April 22, 1884, Sarah became the first Indian woman in American history to appear before Congress when she was called to testify before the House of Representatives Indian Affairs Committee. She told the committee about some of the wrongs her tribe had suffered. She described the government Indian agents such as Rinehart who had gone out of their way to do harm. She wanted her tribe to have a place where families were reunited and provide for themselves their own game, livestock, and crops And she wanted the children to have their own school where they could learn the old ways and the new. In short, she wanted her people to enjoy some of the freedoms and benefits enjoyed by the whites.

Sarah's sincerity moved committee chairman Robert S. Stevens of New York on May 12, 1884, to introduce a bill called "For the Relief of the Paiute Indians." The bill failed to become law.

Real relief for the Paiute would be a long time coming.

Chapter Nine

"Life Among the Piute"

In her lectures and her writing, Sarah described the Paiute way of looking at the world and its people—and, especially, their kindness.

Although strangers often called them savages, the Paiute were a highly spiritual people with a belief system containing many of the same lessons common to the Christianity practiced by the white settlers, as Sarah explained it. Had the whites spent the time to learn about this system, they would have seen how much they had in common with the Paiute, she reasoned.

"But the whites have not waited to find out how good the Indians were," she wrote, "and what ideas they had of God, just like those of Jesus, who called him Father, just as my people do."

There were more lessons that might sound familiar. Paiute were taught not to look down on others. It showed poor character.

"My people teach their children never to make fun of anyone, no matter how they look," Sarah wrote.

And don't hang around in bad company. It reflects poorly on your character.

"If you see your brother or sister doing something wrong, look away, or go away from them," she wrote. "If you make fun of bad persons, you make yourself beneath them."

The Paiute followed something very much like the Golden Rule: "Do unto others as you would have others do unto you. Be kind both to bad and good," she wrote, "for you don't know your own heart. This is the way my people teach their children. It was handed down from father to son for many generations. I never in my life saw our children rude as I have seen white children and grown people in the streets."

As Sarah's friendship with the Boston author and activist Elizabeth Peabody grew, the two found new ways to reach out to the general public in an effort to encourage strangers to show compassion for Native Americans and especially Sarah's Northern Paiute tribe. In 1883, Sarah Winnemucca Hopkins published *Life Among the Piute: Their Wrongs and Claims*. It was the first autobiography ever written by a Native American woman. It was both her personal story and the story of her people.

Like many authors, Sarah received help with her research and editing. Elizabeth Peabody was a prolific writer, the first woman publisher in Boston and even considered the first woman publisher in the US. Her sister, Mary Mann, edited the book and helped with its structure. Sarah's husband, Lewis Hopkins, an educated military man, assisted with research and went all the way to the Library of Congress in Washington, DC to gather material for the project. But it was Sarah's book told in her voice with her unique sense of the world portrayed on every page. And it was a big success.

She started with early childhood memories of her family and the white strangers who passed through Paiute country. At first, Captain Truckee, her influential grandfather, was excited. "My white brothers!" he shouted. "My long-looked for white brothers have come at last!"

The whites passed through for the first few years, but soon came to settle in the area. In harsh winters, Sarah recalled, the Indians gave the newcomers food and did not ask for anything in return.

Sarah wrote about her tribe's spiritual beliefs and described trips she made, illnesses she suffered, the decision to send her to live with the white family of Major Ormsby and learn English in school. Sarah wrote about her respected family and Captain Truckee, her early life, the arrival of the whites, the challenges of learning a new language and seeing the world outside the tribe. From school to the Pyramid Lake and Bannock Wars, she recounted for the first time from an Indian perspective a story that had previously only been told by whites. And, always, she cried out for justice for her people.

When she recounted life on the reservations at Pyramid Lake, Malheur in Oregon, and Yakima, Washington, she incurred the wrath of officials who were supposed to make sure the government's promises made to the Paiute in treaties and laws were kept. Townsfolk often exploited them, and ranchers constantly grazed their cows on reservation land. Promises made to the Paiute were broken, and they often suffered mightily for it.

Under her pen, the Paiute story came to life as never before. In doing so, she made a major contribution to a greater understanding of her people and of all Native Americans. Some scholars believe she also wanted to preserve the memory of her tribe for future generations. The book sold well, reached a wide audience, and she profited from it. She devoted much of the money she made to the education of the tribe's children in the Paiute and white ways, skills that would be essential if they were ever to survive and prosper in the new world.

Chapter Ten

Paying the Price for Speaking Out

Sarah's book was popular and controversial. In some ways it made her more famous than ever. It also made her the target of angry criticism.

Following the printing of her book, Sarah again went to Washington, DC, to speak to members of Congress. She pleaded for help for her people, Nevada's first residents, and on July 6, 1884, legislation was passed that awarded 160 acres to each Paiute family. Although the land was not considered valuable by the whites, after so many years it finally provided places for the Paiute to live in peace.

As Sarah's name and cause grew, so did the efforts to prevent her from reaching her goal of helping her people by speaking out about the troubles they faced. As her people tried to adjust to reservation life, they faced the reality that many benefits that they had been promised were not provided. Those promises were broken only to be replaced by new promises.

It is important to remember that the Paiute and other Native American tribes were not treated as citizens of the United States. They could not vote and were not protected by the rights provided by the US Constitution. In addition, many communities and states had their own "Indian laws" that further discriminated against them. Many Americans at that time considered the Paiute and other Indians little more than savages to be controlled and tamed either by laws or by force.

Sarah's presence in white society as a literate and articulate representative of the tribe was at first a curiosity and then a cause for those who believed Indians deserved respect and better treatment. For some, her continued criticism of the ill treatment her people received from the agents of the Bureau of Indian Affairs became a threat. She would pay a high price by having her personal reputation tarred by those who meant to defeat her cause.

The Council Fire and Arbitrator, a widely circulated Washington-based newspaper published by the Indian Bureau, questioned her honesty, integrity, and morality. Some of the government agents she had attempted to expose for their lack of compassion contributed some of the most vicious attacks against her. They sent copies of their hurtful article to many of the same people who had been contributing to Sarah's cause.

It was a very trying time for Sarah, but she also knew the impact such criticism would have on the Paiute. She was the tribe's only national spokesperson. If white society didn't hear from her and believe her words, they wouldn't hear from any of the Numa.

Fortunately, she also had friends in the press who knew her personally and vouched for her character in articles published in newspapers in Nevada and elsewhere. The *Boston Transcript* wrote, "Sarah Winnemucca (Mrs. Hopkins) has been the object of a villainous attack." Others followed suit.

No response was more powerful than the words published in Winnemucca's *Silver State* newspaper under the headline, "INDIAN BUREAU ALARMED."

"Sarah Winnemucca, the Paiute princess, is lecturing in Boston on what she knows about Indian agents," the story began. "She is throwing hot-shot into the camp of the 'peace policy hypocrites,' who plunder the red man while professing to be his best, truest, and only friend. She knows by practiced experience, acquired at several Indian agencies, that the Indians, with the exception of the head men, are cheated out of their annuities, and not infrequently driven to the warpath by the inhuman treatment of those who are paid by the government to care for their corporeal as well as spiritual wants."

The story defended Sarah's character and reminded readers of her many courageous acts as a scout and interpreter during the Bannock War, serving General O. O. Howard. She had risked her life in a secretive plan that saved many of her own people. She was what one army officer earlier called "perfectly upright and womanly. She is honest, true, faithful, and worthy the respect and esteem of all good people." She had been a teacher and a peacemaker who spoke truth to power—even the all-powerful US government and its corrupt Indian agents. She was willing to call out the "hypocrites, who, while pretending to be the truest friends of the Indians, cheat, starve, and abuse them, and apply the appropriations made by the government for the care of the Indians to their own uses."

Sarah held fast to her belief that the military stationed near the Paiute, not the bureaucrats in far-off Washington, DC, should be put in charge. She believed their training and discipline made them more likely to "deal fairly with them, giving them all that the government appropriates for their use, and holding their chiefs responsible for their good behavior."

Sarah overcame the mean-spirited words from the *Council Fire* and other publications that sought to defame her character and cause.

Long after the vicious voices had been blown away by the desert winds, Sarah's courageous voice would live on in her words.

Chapter Eleven

Teaching Future Generations

Sarah's life bought her fame, but also great frustration. Her book, *Life Among the Paiutes: Their Wrongs and Claims,* opened many eyes to the great difficulties her people faced. But her best efforts to protect and serve her people and communicate their challenges were often unsuccessful. She met with military officers and elected leaders all the way up to the president of the United States to implore them to assist the Paiute people. Many appeared to listen when she argued on her tribe's behalf. But those with the power to help often failed to act.

After speaking before thousands of people from Piper's Opera House in Virginia City, Nevada, to the halls of Congress in Washington, DC, she began to grow weary. As the 1880s wore on, she appeared in public less often. She was in poor health and deeply sad. Even members of her own tribe criticized her. In 1885 she told a reporter for Winnemucca's *Silver State* newspaper that she had battled the government agents for the good of the Paiute, but "as recent events have

Piper's Opera House in Virginia City, Nevada, began attracting
famous stars from all over Europe and the United States in the 1860s.

shown that they are not disposed to stand by me in the
fight, I shall relinquish it."

She turned her focus toward future generations.
If there were a better future for her people, it would
be achieved by the children of the tribe. And to be
prepared for that future, she knew they had to be
educated not only in the Numa way, but in the way of
white society as well.

As early as 1870 Sarah had asked the Indian
authorities to help her start a school to teach the
children. Later at Fort McDermit she tried again. Her
requests were denied. Just as her efforts at Malheur
Reservation as a translator and teacher's assistant to
Annie Parrish were showing promising signs, they were

snubbed by the spiteful William Rinehart. She had even managed to teach at the Yakama Reservation despite its dismal condition.

Once again she sought the help of Elizabeth Peabody, who believed as she did in the necessity of teaching both cultures. Through the years Peabody had helped Sarah in many ways. She was generous with her own money, and she raised funds to support Sarah and the cause of the Paiute. She also wrote and published two in-depth reports to argue that education was the best answer to the Paiute's many challenges: *Sarah Winnemucca's Practical Solution of the Indian Problem (1886)* and *Second Report of the Model School of Sarah Winnemucca (1887)*. She mailed the reports across the country to potential supporters of the cause.

Peabody wrote, "The only vital education that can be given to Indians must be given by Indians themselves who have spoken both languages from childhood, and are able to ground their methods, as she does, in their own inherited natural religion and family moralities."

Sarah would name the school in Elizabeth Peabody's honor.

Sarah wasn't alone in her goal. Other members of her family had their own dreams to better themselves. In 1877, Winnemucca and Natches obtained 160 acres of fertile land at Big Meadows on the Humboldt River outside Lovelock, Nevada. Their goal was to raise enough crops to feed not only themselves and their families, but other Paiute as well. Central

Pacific Railroad railroad magnate and future US senator Leland Stanford of California made the land available through his friendship with Winnemucca lawyer McKaskia "Mac" Bonnifield. Using all the money he and Sarah could gather, Natches was able to buy the land.

Natches and Sarah cleared a place at Big Meadows to build a school that would teach the Paiute children the ways of both the Numa and the white world.

It was a humble place that did not resemble schools elsewhere. Until a proper building could be constructed, she showed progress by building a Paiute brush arbor of sticks, branches, and sagebrush. As the months passed, adobe bricks replaced the brush. A more substantial school took shape with more than two dozen students in attendance. It would also be used for cooking and tribal council meetings.

The children were taught with a patient Paiute hand. Led by Sarah, they learned to march for exercise, "just like soldiers," Lovelock residents thought. They memorized Christian hymns and were taught skills that included sewing. They learned basic arithmetic. Slowly, they learned to comprehend, speak, and read English. Because they were being educated close to home, and not sent to boarding schools many miles away, they were able to remain with their families. This was very important to Sarah.

Townsfolk at first were skeptical that the Paiute could learn, but in time they expressed amazement when they saw the children walking toward the school early each morning, many carrying their lunch "tied in a rag." The Paiute were just like other children, and their hunger to learn changed some hearts and made a positive impact on the community. It can take a long time for some people to see the humanity in those who look different.

Visitors to the school were even more impressed by the students and their teacher. One report recalled, "When we neared the school, shouts of merry laughter ran upon our ears, and little dark and sunburnt faces smile a dim approval of our visitation."

Sarah's own style of teaching also made an impression.

"Speaking in her native tongue, the Princess requested the children name all the visible objects, repeat the days of the week and the months of the year, and calculate to thousands, which they did in a most exemplary manner," one observer wrote. "Then she asked them to give a manifestation of their knowledge upon the blackboard, each in turn printing his name and spelling aloud. It is needless to say, Miss Peabody, that we were spellbound at the disclosure. Nothing but the most assiduous labor could have accomplished this work."

The Lovelock skeptics had been won over. The government, however, was not moved.

At that time, Sarah's teaching method was considered very radical. Education officials then believed that the best way for Native Americans to learn was to erase their heritage and language and teach them to blend, or "assimilate," into white culture. At private boarding schools, children often had their braids cut off and were punished for practicing their spiritual beliefs and otherwise "acting Indian." Perhaps the most famous school to practice the English-only method was the Carlisle Indian Industrial School in Pennsylvania, far from most Indian land.

By 1887 with the passage of the Dawes Act, Indians were further forced to assimilate into white society at the expense of their native culture. Although the Act made it possible for heads of families to receive 160 acres, it opened up the lands for the federal government to sell off at its own profit. What was intended to create independence led to further exploitation.

Sarah's school was successful for a while, but from the start it struggled financially. After the Dawes Act, its days were numbered. It closed in 1889.

Epilogue

Brave Deeds and a Legacy of Hope

When the Peabody school closed, Sarah left Nevada and lived with her sister, Elma, in Idaho. She also spent part of the year in Nevada. She was exhausted and in poor health. Her long, difficult struggle to help her people was almost over. She felt as if she had failed her people.

She once wrote, "With the help of Him who notes the sparrow's fall, I mean to fight for my down-trodden race while life lasts."

In a life in which her people experienced so many broken promises, Sarah kept her promise to live in service of her people even when they shunned her.

Sarah Winnemucca died on October 16, 1891, at Elma's home in Henry's Lake, Idaho. The cause of her death is not fully understood, but it has been reported as both the lung disease tuberculosis and a sudden violent stomach ailment. She died at age forty-seven without fully understanding the important role she had played in the lives of the Paiute and Native Americans everywhere.

Sarah's life was remembered in an article printed on the front page of *The New York Times* on October 27, 1891, in which she was called the "most remarkable woman of the Piutes in Nevada."

She did much to humanize the Paiute in a rapidly changing and often-cruel new world as change swept like wildfire across the West. Many of her best efforts had failed, but her courageous fight against long odds would be long-remembered, become better appreciated with time, and blossom anew as a source of inspiration for future generations.

A century later, after much discussion, Sarah Winnemucca Elementary School was named in her honor in Reno. Today her family name is celebrated at Winnemucca in Humboldt County and Winnemucca Lake (formerly Mud Lake) in her beloved Sierra Nevada. Another dry lake named Winnemucca is located on the Pyramid Lake Indian Reservation. It is home to the oldest petroglyphs in North America. And Sarah's contribution to her people and the history of the state was honored in 2017 by Nevada Governor Brian Sandoval and again in 2019 by Nevada Governor Steve Sisolak, who declared October 16 "Sarah Winnemucca Day."

More than one hundred years after her death, in 2005 a bronze sculpture of Sarah Winnemucca by the renowned artist Benjamin Victor was placed in the National Statuary Hall Collection at the US Capitol in Washington, DC, to honor her role in fighting for

Washoe County School District named an
elementary school after Sarah in Reno, N.V., in 1994.

the rights of the Northern Paiute. She became one
of nine woman in the nation so honored. She joined
Sakakawea of North Dakota as the second Indian
woman to be held in such high esteem.

On the day of the dedication of the statue, Senator
Harry Reid of Nevada said, "It has been written that

Sarah died believing she had not accomplished much—unconvinced that her life had an impact. I think if she could see us today, she might change her mind."

There in the great hall in Washington, DC, the statue of Sarah stands holding in one hand a copy of her important book, *Life Among the Piutes: Their Wrongs and Claims.* In the other hand, she holds up a shell flower forever in bloom.

Oh, Shell Flower, beautiful and strong, how bravely you fought for all the people.

Appendix

In Her Own Words

Sarah Winnemucca's autobiography, *Life Among the Piutes: Their Wrongs and Claims,* tells the incredible story of her upbringing and fight for the rights of her people. Here are some excerpts:

On her fear of the newcomers: "Very late that fall, my father and grandfather and a great many more went down to the Humboldt River to fish. They brought back a great many fish, which we were very glad to get; for none of our people had been down to fish the whole summer.

"When they came back, they brought us more news. They said there were some white people living at the Humboldt sink. They were the first ones my father had seen face to face. He said they were not like 'humans.' They were more like owls than anything else. They had hair on their faces, and had white eyes, and looked beautiful.

"I tell you we children had to be very good, indeed, during the winter; for we were told that if we were not good they would come and eat us up."

On entering a settler's home for the first time and seeing

tables and chairs: "Oh, what pretty things met my eyes. I was looking all around the room, and I saw beautiful white cups, and every beautiful thing on something high and long, and around it some things that were red.

"I said to my sister, 'Do you know what those are?' for she had been to the house before with my mother and brothers. She said, 'That high thing is what they use when eating, and the white cups are what they drink hot water from, and the red things you see is what they sit upon when they are eating.' There was one now near us, and I thought if I could sit upon it I should be so happy! I said to my mother, 'Can I sit on that one?' She said, 'No, they would whip you.' I did not say any more, but sat looking at the beautiful chair."

On recalling her Numa name, Thocmetony, and the song she sang as a young girl: "I, Sarah Winnemucca, am a shell-flower, such as I wear on my dress. My name is Thocmetony. I am so beautiful! Who will come and dance with me while I am so beautiful? Oh, come and be happy with me! I shall be beautiful while the earth lasts."

On being frustrated in her effort to help her people: "When I went to Carson City in 1870 to see about my people's affairs, I was sent by the officials from one to another. At last we went to San Francisco to see General Schofield, and he sent me back to see Senator Jones. So brother and I went to where he was living in Gold Hill. He said, 'I will see to it.' He then put into my hands twenty dollars, which I took gratefully, for we were always poor, and brother and I went away. I have never seen or heard from him since."

On the simple and pure understanding of the Paiute people: "My people are ignorant of worldly knowledge, but they know what love means and what truth means. They have seen their dear ones perish around them because their white brothers have given them neither love nor truth. Are not love and truth better than learning? My people have no learning. They do not know anything about the history of the world, but they see the Spirit-Father in everything. The beautiful world talks to them of their Spirit-Father. They are innocent and simple, but they are brave and will not be imposed upon. They are patient, but they know black is not white."

Glossary and Key Characters in This Story

Bannock—a group of Native Americans who lived in
Oregon and Idaho.

Captain Truckee—The leader of the Northern Paiute
and Sarah Winnemucca's maternal grandfather. He
befriended Captain John C. Frémont, who gave him
the title "Captain."

Chief Winnemucca—Leader of the Northern Paiute after
the death of his father-in-law, Captain Truckee.
Winnemucca was Sarah's father.

Hayes, Rutherford B.—US President (1877–1881). He met
briefly with Sarah to discuss the problems of the
Northern Paiute.

Humboldt River—Nevada's longest river at almost 300
miles. Northern Paiute lived near the Humboldt and
fished its waters for hundreds of years before settlers
came to the area.

Manos—a round stone often gathered from a river used to
grind seeds into meal.

Metate—a larger stone used as a grinding bowl.

Numa—"The people," the name the Northern Paiute called
themselves.

Ormsby, Major William - Former Major in the Pennsylvania
militia, leading figure in Nevada, died in Py

Pyramid Lake—A desert lake located in northwestern

63

Nevada with a pyramid-shaped island and 115,000-acre surface. Its deepest point is 360 feet. The Northern Paiute fished its waters for many generations.

Reservation—Land set aside by the government as a home for Native Americans. Pyramid Lake, Malheur, and Yakima are three examples of reservations.

Shoshone—Native American tribe with members in Nevada, Utah, Idaho, and Wyoming.

Sierra Nevada—Mountain range that stretches hundreds of miles and created a western boundary for the Northern Paiute.

Thocmetony—"Thoc-met-ony." The birth name of the girl who became known as Sarah Winnemucca. It means "Shell Flower."

Tuboitony—"Tube-wa-tony." The name of Sarah Winnemucca's mother. She was killed by soldiers in 1865 at what became known as the Mud Lake Massacre.

Tule Reed—A stiff grass that grows in marshes and by lakes. Used by the Northern Paiute to make skirts, sandals, and baskets.

Selected Bibliography and Further Reading

Carpenter, Cari M., and Carolyn Sorisio, eds. *The Newspaper Warrior: Sarah Winnemucca Hopkins' Campaign for American Indian Rights, 1864-1991.* Lincoln: University of Nebraska Press, 2015.

Cleere, Jan. *More Than Petticoats: Remarkable Nevada Women.* Guilford, Conn.: The Globe Pequot Press, 2005.

Egan, Ferol. *Sand in a Whirlwind: The Paiute Indian War of 1860.* Garden City, NY: Doubleday & Co., 1972.

Forbes, Jack. *Native Americans of California and Nevada.* Happy Camp, Calif.: Naturegraph Publishers, 1982.

Gehm, Katherine. *Sarah Winnemucca: Most Extraordinary Woman of the Paiute Nation.* Phoenix: O'Sullivan Woodside & Co., 1975.

Hulse, James W. *The Silver State: Nevada's Heritage Reinterpreted.* Reno: University of Nevada Press, 1991.

Jackson, Helen H. *A Century of Dishonor.* New York: Harper & Brothers, 1881.

Knack, Martha C., and Omer C. Stewart. *As Long as the River Shall Run: An Ethnohistory of Pyramid Lake Indian Reservation.* Reno: University of Nevada Press, 1984.

Seagraves, Anne. *High-Spirited Women of the West.* Hayden, Idaho: Wesanne Publications, 1992.

Turner, Erin H., Editor. *Wise Women: From Pocahontas to Sarah Winnemucca, Remarkable Stories of Native American*

Trailblazers. Guilford, CT: The Globe Pequot Press, 2009.

Whitney Canfield, Gae. *Sarah Winnemucca of the Northern Paiutes.* Norman: University of Oklahoma Press, 1983.

Winnemucca Hopkins, Sarah. *Life Among the Piutes: Their Wrongs and Claims.* Reno: University of Nevada Press, 1994. Originally published in 1883.

Zanjani, Sally. *Sarah Winnemucca.* Lincoln, Neb.: Bison Books, 2004.

Blog: Library of Congress. "Native American Heritage Month: Celebrating Sarah Winnemucca, 2017. https://blogs.loc.gov/loc/2017/11/native-american-heritage-month-celebrating-sarah-winnemucca/

Questions for Discussion

1. What do you think made Sarah Winnemucca special?
2. What was the importance of Sarah's friendship with Lizzie Ormsby?
3. What fears did Sarah have to overcome to help her people?
4. What did Sarah think of the importance of education?
5. How did Sarah communicate to large groups?
6. How were the Northern Paiute and the settlers alike?
7. How did the Northern Paiute stay warm in winter, and why did they move around so much?
8. How did Nevada's climate and landscape impact the Northern Paiute and the settlers?
9. What was the importance of Pyramid Lake and the Humboldt River in the lives of the Northern Paiute?
10. What was the effect of the discovery of gold and silver in the region on the living conditions of the Northern Paiute?
11. What was the importance of the publication of Sarah Winnemucca's book, *Life Among the Piutes: Their Wrongs and Claims*?

About the Author

Native Nevadan John L. Smith is a longtime journalist and the author of more than a dozen books. He has won many state, regional, and national awards for his writing and was inducted into the Nevada Press Association Newspaper Hall of Fame in 2016, the same year that saw him honored with the James Foley/Medill Medal for Courage in Journalism, the Society of Professional Journalists Ethics Award, and the Ancil Payne Award for Ethics in Journalism from the University of Oregon. He freelances for a variety of publications, including *The Nevada Independent.* The father of a grown daughter, Amelia, he is married to the writer Sally Denton and makes his home in Boulder City, Nevada.